Get the Interview & Get the Job!

In-side secrets from an In-house Recruiter!

Dawn Moss MCIPD

Tap into over a decade of experience, knowledge, skills and the odd anecdote!

Improve your chances of being selected for an interview and securing that job with my step by step easy to understand interview guide.

First Published in 2014
Printed and bound by Amazon createspace
Designed by Pixel Studios: http://www.fiverr.com/pixelstudio
This book is printed on demand so no copies will be remaindered or
pulped – responsible printing.

ISBN-13 978-1499579840
ISBN-10 1499579845

Table of Contents

7   **Introduction**

How this book is structured

11   **Chapter One ~ Job Hunting Strategies**

Job Hunting Strategies

Where do you start to look for your ideal job?

How to Manage Your Recruitment Consultant

35   **Chapter Two ~ Compelling Cover Letters**

Cover Letter – Why bother in this age of technology!

47   **Chapter Three ~ Write a winning Curriculum Vitae**

The Basics

CV Checklist

Hot top tips from the experts!

57   **Chapter Four ~ Preparation before the Interview**

The Job Description

The Job Advert

The Company Website

65   Chapter Five ~ Types of Interviews

Unstructured Interviews

Panel Interviews

Assessment Centres

Telephone Interviews

Psychometric Testing

81   Chapter Six ~ Motivational Fit

Job Fit

Organisational & Corporate Culture Fit

87   Chapter Seven ~ Commonly Asked Questions

Top Ten Common Questions

General Questions to consider

97   Chapter Eight ~ Behavioural Competency Style Interviews & Questions

Introduction to Behavioural Competencies

What, Why, and How of using behavioural competency style interviews.

Using the S.T.A.R. Model to prepare

125 **Chapter Nine ~ How to Market your Value Proposition**

How to Market your Value Proposition

129 **Chapter Ten ~ Avoid the Common Mistakes**

Avoid Common Mistakes

137 **Chapter Eleven ~ Offer Stage**

Negotiating the Offer

149 **Conclusion**

151 **About the Author**

153 **Acknowledgements**

154 **Resources & Useful Links**

Introduction

Hiring the right people, with the right skills at the right time is fundamental for business success today and they are looking for talent like you!

I recently heard that having a business with no advertising is like dating in the dark – you can spend all night smiling but no one will see you!!

It's similar when you are looking for a job – if you are not out there marketing yourself in the right places it's like jumping up and down and shouting in the middle of the forest – no one is going to see or hear you!

Going through the recruitment process is a game and one you have to take seriously every time and approach with a winning mind set. After all there are no prizes for second place! You have to think confidently and think you are going to win every single time you apply for a vacancy. There is no place for a half hearted approach in this game otherwise someone else is going to reap the rewards.

This book will make the whole process very simple to understand and walk you through step by step.

How this book is structured

Chapter One is all about creating long term **Job Hunting Strategies** to satisfy your career aspirations and ensure you focus your valuable time and effort on developing a tailored search.

Chapter Two helps you understand why it's still important to write a **Compelling Cover Letter** even in this age of technology. This chapter also helps point out the important elements to include on a good cover letter and compel an employer to want to interview you!

Chapter Three helps you **Write a Winning CV** in order to stand out from the hundreds of applications received by popular organisations. It's essential you make a good and quick impression with a clear and concise CV.

Chapter Four explains the different **Types of Interviews** you can expect and in turn will help you prepare appropriately.

Chapter Five is dedicated to the importance of **Motivational Fit** and explains what managers and recruiters look out for during the interview process and the pieces of information they gather to make decisions about your motivational fit.

Chapter Six outlines how important it is to prepare for different types of interviews and equally important to understand and prepare for **Commonly asked Questions.** In this chapter we will give you some information to consider when preparing for these questions.

Chapter Seven is a very important chapter and one worth reading a couple of times to **Understand and Prepare for Behavioural Competency Interviews** because using this information could give you the edge over other candidates that generalise and make vague statements.

Chapter Eight explains the opposite side of Employer Proposition and shows you **How you can Market your Value Proposition** to the organisation. Learn how to present an attractive and valuable proposition during the interview.

Chapter Nine helps you to understand and **Avoid Common Mistakes** made by other candidates and prepare accordingly.

Chapter Ten gives you some information and support for the all important **Offer Stage.** This chapter gives you some tips on how to negotiate the offer.

CHAPTER ONE

Job Hunting Strategies

Job Hunting Strategies

Before we launch into talking about how to manage your current search and where to look for your ideal job let's talk about if you are at the consideration stage or just thinking about your next move.

We tend to leave our job search for when we are looking for a job – yes makes sense, it's a logical plan of action. However, if you know you will not stay in one job for life then it makes more sense to build a job hunting strategy before it becomes a necessity or you're desperate and no one likes to be desperate!!

It's easy to get comfortable in a role – like an old pair of slippers! Should a job be like a warm, cosy, pair of slippers? No challenge, no stretch targets, no development to me equals de-motivation, lack of productivity and lack of personal progression.

Don't leave it too late to implement your job searching strategies for your future career (within your current organisation or externally). Act while you are relatively content but hungry for the next challenge or promotion.

If it looks and feels like there will not be any progression or promotional opportunities for you in the future, you should seriously consider if this is the place you want to retire!

Getting complacent in your job is a slow, painful experience for you, the boss, and your colleagues and for the business – it can be toxic for your career plan, sapping your energy enthusiasm and self esteem.

If you lose focus and concentration – BE WARNED this state can also sabotage your next career move as you'll carry that resentment or bitterness and lethargy into the interview and it isn't pretty!

---

1. Network, Network….and then Do Some More Networking!

Networking should form part of your continuous development plan ("CDP") throughout the duration of your career (whether you are in a job or own a business). Don't just pick up with people when you need their support.

Be prepared to put in some time, effort and a little ground work prior to looking for a new job or even starting a business before you ask for that "favour!" or ask for a recommendation on LinkedIn.

The key to networking should be mutually beneficial – yes you could use the old term "you scratch my back and I'll scratch yours" but I was trying to bring networking into the 21st century. "You recommend me and I'll recommend you" or "You endorse my skills and knowledge…" You get the point. Meet with people that will enhance your career, knowledge and give you an opportunity to understand the trends and updates in that industry.

Just Network! I was chatting to my mortgage advisor recently about my business plan and he gave me a potential lead – so it's good to talk…to everyone!

---

2. Social Media Networking

LinkedIn, Twitter and Facebook (follow me!) are particularly good business networking tools – in fact the internet is fantastic for finding out information about anything and everything and has such a wider reaching capability.

Try the "get introduced" feature on LinkedIn if you are particularly interested in joining or finding out more about an organisation. This is valuable information we just wouldn't have had without

Social Media – now you know who to network with and how.

Networking can take place on the internet however this shouldn't be your only method of building a long term and trusted relationship. Social media should not be ignored or avoided as it is a very powerful tool for lots of reasons.

Virtual networking is definitely okay these days and you can build relationships with your customers by providing good quality information and content on your website, blogs, and posts. It's a great method of engaging with a wider audience and your potential prospects.

---

3. Research & Regularly Read the News in Your Sector

This has several benefits to your existing career and any future interview or career – keeping up to date with the latest legislation, regulation changes, competition, trends, forecasts can mean getting the job or not.

If you are portraying yourself as the "Expert" in your field you better be up to date – it's going to be awkward and embarrassing to miss an important change in the industry and be caught out!

Dedicate some time every day to reading the professional journals, relevant newspapers, or sign up to news updates in your sector. If you are a regular commuter then this is an ideal time to read the latest news in your industry and you can always nap on the journey home!

---

4. Keep Your CV & On-Line Profile Up to Date

It's so much easier if you keep your CV up to date, rather than struggling to put something together from scratch, quickly and then realising you've missed some important information or an achievement. Particularly if you have been in the same role for a number of years – you will forget some information that could mean you getting invited to interview or not.

Your CV is extremely important in your job search and keeping your on-line profile up to date is part of that commitment to your career development.

Get into the habit of keeping it updated – otherwise if you leave it dormant for years and then start updating your profile this could raise suspicions with your current employer or other team members.

All of your actions on-line are recorded….and some are announced to the world! Be careful what you do on-line. This is why it's so important to regularly maintain your profile; it then becomes part of your routine and no one will ask awkward questions when you start job searching.

---

5. Keep the End in Mind

What's your career goal? Where do you want to take your career? What's your game plan?

If you don't know where you are going…you'll end up somewhere else! You may as well hand over your career for someone else to make the decisions.

I've interviewed many candidates over the last six years who don't have a career plan – they are conveniently blaming or justifying not having a plan because how can you possibly have a plan in these economic times and this rotten labour market!

No one said you couldn't have a flexible plan but you wouldn't jump on the first bus or train and not check whether it was going in vaguely the direction you wanted to eventually end up.

Having a plan means you are selective and this will go in your favour when you are in the interview. Managers will know if you are genuinely interested in working in their team – well thought out reasons for applying for their job and wanting to work in the team.

Think about your motivation for the job, motivation for the organisation and how you fit with the culture, values, and core principles. Remember motivation needs to be a two way process – both you and the organisation need to benefit.

You need to be able to contribute immediately but be given the opportunity to develop or improve new and existing skills and knowledge.

That's the same for the organisation – they need immediate productivity and an employee engaged and motivated to learn more.

6. Learn Something New or Refresh Your Existing Skills – Join A Club or Register for a Workshop.

Another good way of networking with other like minded people and learn at the same time is to join a class, workshop, training session, webinar or seminar (the list is endless) – it may even contribute to your CDP for your particular sector, HR, Accountancy, Lawyers etc.

Joining a professional association is another great way of networking, learning about the latest in your industry and provides a socialising opportunity. This is networking at its best – because you're not under pressure to sell yourself or desperate for that next job. This is an opportunity to build up a longer term relationship with people in your field.

7. Pre-Sell Yourself!

This is a very well documented internet product launch tactic and a strategy used for building customer anticipation and engagement – so why not adapt and use the same strategy for yourself.

This really means at every opportunity be positive about yourself, your skills, knowledge, the organisations you've worked with and for and remember keep the end goal in mind.

Be your most professional self at events, seminars and training programmes. You never know when your next manager or client will be in the room. Thinking long term is essential – so don't go straight in for the sale!

There is an art to selling yourself and this is one of the most important reasons for investing time and energy keeping those key relationships up to date.

Everything you do and everything you say counts in work and business. This includes your internet chat, every comment and tweet you post on-line.

Okay let's move on to actually looking for the next job and how you are going to manage your job hunting strategies.

Don't just think about the next move – think a little longer term and plan out the steps or moves or job positions that will take you in the right direction.

If you think short term you may select jobs that are not suitable or won't contribute to the longer term aspirations.

It's a little more difficult to explain moves that don't make sense to your longer term career.

Where do you start to look for your ideal job?

So you've started your job hunting search and you've found hundreds, if not thousands of results on Google!

1. Keep calm and focused on your objective or ideal job, industry or particular organisation.

2. Focus on the sector or specialist subject you are interested. Narrow your efforts initially and keep the search to a particular industry.

3. Focus on how you are going to apply - direct, speculatively, via Social Media, Networking, or through a specialist agency.

Keep Focused

Plan your job hunting and at first keep your search contained and narrow - you can widen your search later if you are not getting the desired results. However, always think long term and select roles that will keep you moving and progressing in the right direction.

Consider which organisations you would like to work and approach direct. Review the top 100 places to work at The Sunday Times.

Just reviewing this list of companies will give you other ideas of where you would like to work - Banking, Financial Services, Construction, Retail, Marketing, Media, Hospitality, Sports & Leisure, etc.

It's not good to spray your CV across a broad range – you'll lose track of where you've applied and this will go against you if employers find out your interest is shallow.

Keep a Record

This is an important point here – you don't want to apply for the same job several times or get submitted by an agency twice!

If you work in a particularly small niche market – your reputation is important and you want to act professionally during your search as well as the interview.

If you annoy or upset people trying to support your application you may not get an interview at all. The good consultants will have very good relationships with their clients and as you know bad news travels faster than good news!

Keep Trying

Be persistent without being a nuisance in your job hunting activities and communication.

Again it's worth keeping a note of when you last got in contact with your recruitment consultant to make sure you are keeping your name in the frame however, not getting a name because you pester.

Keep Positive & Patient

I understand first-hand what it's like job hunting and searching for that ideal job and being very disheartened when you keep receiving the "no thanks" letter or call.

Try not to dwell on the rejections and move on and focus on getting back to the search. This job just wasn't for you this time. The next opportunity may be a better job anyway – so keep going and leave the past where it belongs!

Keep an Open Mind

Don't just restrict your search with the big high street stores (Monster, Totaljobs, eFinancial Careers). These are obviously very powerful big brands and definitely use these to search for jobs and also register your CV and set up job alerts.

However, don't forget the smaller niche agency that specialise in your chosen field. If you are particularly focused on the IT industry go to a specialist like NDK Consultants or HR Specialists like Oakleaf Partners or G Square HR.

These types of agents normally have to work very hard building up and maintaining their networks and relationships and have to continually demonstrate their ability to meet the needs of their clients.

On the flip side they don't have a huge client range and will not have lots of vacancies at any one time. So always combine your search with several agencies.

Keep to the basics

It's good practice to keep your CV up to date even when you are not looking for a job. You want to be ready to apply.

Make sure you highlight the skills, knowledge and the experience relevant for the job you are applying.

Keep Networking

In today's world of advanced technology it's easy to network on-line through various social media channels, LinkedIn, Twitter & Facebook.

However, don't forget to network in person - attend seminars, and breakfast meetings, even if you know a topic or subject well.

It's good to keep in contact in person and then when you do need support you'll have lots of options.

How to Manage your Recruitment Consultant

Part of your job hunting plan may include registering with Recruitment Agencies. Here are some tips on how to manage your Recruitment Consultant.

If you are in the process of looking for your next job, new to using a recruitment agency, a graduate looking for your first job, or new to the UK job market then this next section - 5 R's to managing your Recruitment Agency could help you make the journey of managing your consultant a little easier and effective.

1. Responsibility

Your career and job search are your responsibility. It's your responsibility to manage your applications and manage your career.

Let's talk a little about your recruitment consultants' job. The main purpose and the most important one to remember, is the recruitment consultants job is to generate revenue for the agency. It's not purely to seek out and find opportunities to place you in your perfect job.

They are mainly interested in filling the vacancies that they receive from their clients. To some extent they will "spec" you into a company – this will be either by random emails to companies they don't even work with or cold calling.

2. Right people, right job, right time

We all know the importance of timing! Your agent can only be as effective on your behalf if they have the vacancies at the time you contact them – otherwise you'll end up on their database waiting for the right opportunity to pop up.

For this reason you need to keep in contact with your consultant – make sure you get the balance right here otherwise you'll be known for all the wrong reasons.

Agree with your consultant to keep in regular contact and agree the method preferred.

3. Register

We've already mentioned the main purpose of a recruitment consultant is to generate revenue. They may also have lots of other measured targets, number of cold calls, number of meetings with prospective clients, candidates they place into interview and the one you will be most interested – registering candidates.

Be mindful and selective about which agencies you register with. Registering can mean taking valuable time out to visit the agents' offices, fill out their application forms and be interviewed with the consultant. If you are working this is your time or your annual leave.

You may wish to ask a few questions before registering with many agencies (What types of clients do you work with? Do you have the types of jobs I'm looking for?).

Ensure the agency you register with can assist in your search for the right job. Are they working with the sector or industry you are interested in?

Consider every interaction with the consultant as an interview – they will be forming a professional opinion of you every time you call or meet – so treat it as a practise interview.

The consultants may have very good and long term relationships with their clients and they will not want to represent someone who will damage this working relationship.

4. Record & Review

It's essential to keep detailed and accurate records – particularly if you are going to register with lots of different agencies. You will forget which agency is representing you for which job and that may reflect in your interviews – you may even get sent forward twice to the client (your prospective employer!).

This situation is time consuming and rather annoying in the recruitment process (for both the recruitment consultant and the client).

You don't want to damage your reputation in the market before you've even met the interviewers. Depending on your sector or industry it can be a very small market.

5. Respect

Learn to manage your consultant and understand they have a high pressured and sometimes stressful job. Keep your consultant up to date with your other interviews; it's the polite, nice and courteous thing to do. However, there's no need to tell them every detail such as where and who you are interviewing with.

Of course they will want you to disclose this information but be mindful and ask yourself why they would want to know who. Remind yourself of their role – to generate revenue, sign up new clients and register new candidates.

Once they have this information from you they will probably cold call that company and try to submit other candidates – is more competition what you need at the moment?

Always return the agent's calls - don't just disappear without a trace! This again is basic courtesy. You want to maintain a good relationship in case you need their help again in the future and remember it's a small market!

Recommended Recruitment Agencies:

- NDK
- G Square HR
- Prime Personnel
- Robert Walters
- Morgan McKinley
- Hays
- Robert Half
- Top Flight Personnel
- Reed
- Adecco & Office Angels

On-Line Job Boards

- eFinancial Careers - Financial Sector
- Monster - General
- Reed - Administration / Office
- Totaljobs - General
- The Lawyer - Legal Sector
- Personnel Today - Human Resources Sector☐
- Indeed – General

Write down three actions to kick start your job search:

_____

_____

_____

_____

_____

_____

_____

_____

_____

_____

_____

CHAPTER TWO

Compelling Cover Letters

Compelling Cover Letters

We live in a quick and instant world today – emails are sent in fractions of a second, tweets are no more than 140 characters and text talk is just gr8t!

So it would be understandable that taking a traditional approach to applying for a job is viewed as a bit dated! Who writes letters these days!?! Can you tell me the price of a first class stamp? Why bother writing a cover letter?

Put your personal opinions aside as employers still expect a well presented and well written Cover Letter and CV – even if it's attached to an email!

Here are the main reasons why you should bother to write a tailored cover letter with every application.

First Impressions Count

A Cover Letter and CV are your opportunity to make that all important first impression with a company or organisation. We all know that first impressions count and it's the same with a cover letter.

If you have not made much effort – then don't expect anyone else to. If you haven't taken the time to polish and tailor the letter then how can you expect others to take the time to read or review?

I know it must be disheartening to be rejected and keep your enthusiasm when applying but be persistent and learn to put the past behind you and focus on moving forward positively.

Time & Effort Gets Results

Taking the time and making the effort to write a cover letter from scratch demonstrates you are genuinely interested in the organisation.

If you have a standard plain vanilla cover letter it gives the impression that you are possibly throwing CVs randomly – anywhere and everywhere!!

I've been an in-house recruiter for many years and have received some very poor cover letters or no cover letter at all – even candidates that had forgotten to change the company name they wanted so much to work for.....it wasn't the same company I worked for!!

Does this inspire people to take this relationship any further – no!

On-Line Etiquette

You may well ask why bother with a Cover Letter when you are sending your application by email? I've received many emails with just the CV attached – the candidates have not even bothered to write an email.

There is still an expectation that people will follow basic etiquette on-line. It's generally viewed as bad manners not to write a Cover Letter even if it's on the email itself.

How you behave throughout the application process will tell the employer a lot about your attitude to going the extra mile – if you don't make the necessary effort and take the time at this crucial stage then it's allowing negative assumptions to be made.

Highlight Relevant Information

If you have taken the time to write the cover letter to match the requirements and highlight your skills, knowledge and experience this also demonstrates you have read the advertisement and understand the criteria for the job.

There are lots of candidates that apply for jobs when they don't match the essential criteria. So don't be put off when you see the number of applications to a certain job vacancy – they won't all match the criteria. Some are trying their luck or think they could get spotted for another vacancy.

Unfortunately, they are probably wasting their time – recruiters often deal with 100s of applications for one job and if you don't match the criteria for this job your CV is likely to be filed and rarely viewed or visited again…sorry!

Research the Company

Research the company just as you would if you were invited to an interview. Write a short paragraph to explain a couple of reasons for being interested in that organisation and back up those reasons. It's not enough to use general statements like "the company has a good reputation in the market" or "I want to work for an International or Global company" these are too vague and look like a copy and paste job!

Let them know why you think these are important aspects – "I want to work for an International Company to be able to fully utilise my language capabilities and long term I would like to expand my knowledge and experience globally."

Write Compelling Cover Letters

It's one of the first documents you will draft after your CV when you see that interesting vacancy.

You'll be under pressure to apply within the deadline so take extra care and make sure it's accurate.

No silly typos or spelling mistakes and your grandma is okay.....what's my grandma got to do with covering letters.......oh sorry grammar!

The Basics

- Name
- Address
- Telephone numbers - Land Line & Mobile
- Email address
- Where you saw the job advertised

There are no requirements to include date of birth, marital status or numbers of children.

These questions should not be asked during the recruitment process as they are unlawful under the Equality Act 2010.

Reasons for Applying

It's really important you take the time to explain why you have applied for this role. Explain your reasons for being attracted to the job and the company. Remember how important employers rank motivation for the job.

Include your reasons for wanting to join that organisation. This means a little preparation is required. Review the company's website and focus your time on key information: CEO Speech, Vision, Mission, Core Values, Products, Services and any recent news articles.

Relevant Information

Highlight relevant information:

- Skills

- Knowledge

- Types of Experience

However don't just put all the information from your CV onto the Letter. Keep it clear and concise!

Mind the Gaps

Ensure you explain the gaps (if any) in your employment history. You may well have a good reason, however it's better to explain rather than leave it for the reader to guess!

Reasons for Leaving

We've talked about reasons for applying - you may want to outline your reasons for leaving or starting to look for another job. Be careful here....don't be negative about your current or last employer.

Keep Clear & Concise

Keep it clear and concise - this is not the time to tell your story in full! Just give some edited highlights relevant to the job.

Type or Write

Type the letter unless asked to write.

Even if you are sending a CV on-line it's courteous to type or attach a cover letter - not just throw the CV onto a blank email!

Yes I still receive emails like that today - it's not professional and it's a little rude.

Jargon & Acronyms

Avoid using jargon and acronyms unless it's widely used or known in the general market - note it may not be the recruiting manager reading your application, it may be someone in HR and they won't necessarily know what the industry jargon means.

Mrs. S. Cotton
Senior HR Business Partner
ABC Bank
83 The High Road,
Colchester, CO1

Ms D Moss
Colchester, Essex.
07932 434 303
Email

27th May 2014

Dear Ms Cotton,

Application - Human Resources Manager

Following your recent advert in the Colchester Gazette for the Human Resources Manager position it immediately captured my interest. I am confident that my solid experience provides me with the capabilities to successfully fill this position. Accordingly I have enclosed my curriculum vitae for your consideration.

Here are some skills and achievements that I would bring to the job:

- 10 years coaching and advising senior management on employee issues at XXX organisation
- Responsible for recruitment and selection of over X employees at all levels in the organisation
- Designed and implemented a staff retention program that resulted in a 10% improvement in employee retention
- Successfully introduced a performance management system throughout the organisation
- Successful implementation of a career path management program
- In depth knowledge and understanding of employment law and legislation to ensure compliance

I am seeking an opportunity to excel in a dynamic company and I am confident of the contribution I can make to ABC Bank. I would welcome the opportunity to meet with you to further discuss this opportunity.

Please contact me, via phone or e-mail, to set up a mutually convenient time and date for us to meet. Thank you for your time and consideration.

Yours sincerely,

Cover Letter – Example:

[NAME OF RECRUITER]
[TITLE OF RECRUITER]
[NAME OF COMPANY]
[ADDRESS]

[YOUR NAME]
[YOUR ADDRESS]
[YOUR PHONE NO:]
[YOUR EMAIL]

[INSERT DATE]

Dear [INSERT NAME OF RECRUITER],

Application – [INSERT JOB TITLE]

Following your recent advert in the [INSERT WHERE YOU SAW THE JOB ADVERT] for the above position it immediately captured my interest. I am confident that my skills and knowledge provides me with the capabilities to successfully fill this position. Accordingly I have enclosed my curriculum vitae for your consideration.

Here are some skills and achievements that I would bring to the job:

- [INSERT REASONS FOR HIRING YOU]
- [INSERT SKILLS & EXPERIENCES MATCHING THE CRITERIA OF THE VACANCY APPLIED]
- [INSERT SKILLS & EXPERIENCES MATCHING THE CRITERIA OF THE VACANCY APPLIED]
- [INSERT SKILLS & EXPERIENCES MATCHING THE CRITERIA OF THE VACANCY APPLIED]

I am seeking an opportunity to [INSERT YOUR MOTIVATIONAL REASONS AND WHY YOU ARE ATTRACTED TO THE JOB AND ORGANISATION]. I would welcome the opportunity to meet with you to further discuss this opportunity.

Please contact me, via phone or e-mail, to set up a mutually convenient time and date for us to meet. Thank you for your time and consideration.

Yours sincerely,

[INSERT YOUR NAME]

Write a few notes on building a cover letter template – what are you going to include:

_____

_____

_____

_____

_____

_____

_____

_____

_____

_____

_____

CHAPTER THREE

Write a Winning Curriculum Vitae

Write a Winning CV - How to stand out from the Competition!

If you are staring at a blank Word document and just don't know where to start with writing your curriculum vitae....stay calm help is at hand!

Here are the six basics building blocks that should appear on your CV

1. **Contact Information**, Address, Telephone Numbers, Email address etc.
2. **Personal Statement** - include some general statements that describe you as a person, and your career aspirations.
3. **Education & Qualifications** - School, College, University etc.
4. **Certificates & Training** - particularly relevant to the job you are applying.
5. **Job / Employment History** (include start and finish dates, job title, main tasks and duties and achievements)
6. **Achievements** - this is so important that I've mentioned it twice! This is where you can back up all those general statements. See below for some ideas or suggestions.

Here are some examples of descriptive sentences to help you create that winning CV

- Assisted the Senior Management team

- Supported the business with the smooth running of....

- Designed a training session for Senior Managers

- Implemented a new system / process to manage the payments

- Responsible for the South East sales team

- Accountable for the teams budget

- Created the communications plan for the promotion of.....

- Managed the process / function.....

- Provided expertise advice on all legal aspects....

Here are some questions to ask yourself when you are writing up your achievements

- How did your involvement save time, money or both for the organisation?

- Did you solve a particular problem and describe the steps you took to solve?

- How did you increase the profitability of the organisation?

- Describe when you created new revenue generating channels?

- Describe the implementation of a new system or process?

- When did you use your initiative to make positive changes, save time or money?

- Did you implement a training workshop or design a training session?

Here are some personal statement examples

School Leavers

A highly motivated and hardworking individual, who has recently completed their A-Levels, achieving excellent grades in both Maths and English.

Seeking an apprenticeship in the [name the sector, Engineering, Retail, Leisure & Tourism, Pharmaceutical, Banking, Financial Services, Marketing etc.] to build upon an interest in XXX and start a career as a XXX.

Ultimate career goal is to become a fully-qualified and experienced XXX, with the longer-term aspiration of moving into XXX.

Graduates

A recent business economics and finance graduate with a 2:1 honours degree from the University of X, looking to secure a Graduate Analyst position to use and further develop my analytical skills and knowledge in a practical and fast-paced environment.

My career goal is to assume a role which allows me to take responsibility for the analysis and interpretation of commercial and financial data for a well respected and market leading organisation.

Here are some general statements

- Results driven - methodical approach to achieving tasks and objectives

- Determined and decisive, uses initiative to develop effective solutions to problems

- Reliable and dependable

- High degree of accuracy and attention to detail

- Pro-active - strong personal drive to achieve

- Identifies and develops opportunities – innovative and makes things happen

- Good strategic appreciation and vision - able to build and implement strategic plans

- Strives for quality and applies process and discipline towards maximising performance

- Extremely reliable and dependable

- Analytical, inquisitive and comfortable with using different questioning techniques

- Methodical approach to planning and organising - good at managing time and resources

CV Check List

- Does the layout and format of your CV look and feel professional?
- Is it interesting to read?
- Will it get the reader's attention?
- Is the style of writing clear and concise?
- Is the style consistent throughout the CV?
- Don't include too many different bullet points, or fonts or make the CV too busy – keep it simple
- Make sure your employment history is written in reverse chronological order – with your current or most recent job listed on the first page.
- Always include a Cover Letter with your CV - even if you're sending it by email.
- Avoid wide margins at the side of the page
- Double check and triple check for spelling mistakes – don't rely on your computer to pick up spelling or grammar errors – there, their, they're – all spelt right, write, rite but have different meanings!
- After you've checked the spelling ask a good friend to check too.

Hot Top Tips from the Experts!

- Put your achievements (relevant to the job you are applying) on the first page of your CV.
- Employers these days look for commercial awareness – so make sure you include the facts and figures with your achievements.
- Always include your language skills – don't assume the interviewer will guess you have another language!
- Don't write "CV" at the top of the page - we know it's a CV there's no need to waste a line by stating the obvious.
- Include your name in the footer on every single page of the CV - Recruiters are often interrupted (a lot!!) in their jobs, clients visiting their desks, phone calls, colleagues needing quick updates on vacancies etc. So if your CV is printed off and the pages get detached from each other the recruiter will still have your name.
- Don't have too much white space on the page - this is a waste of space and could be used to communicate additional and useful information on one page.

- Don't tell a story - Recruiters especially don't have the time to read loads of information.
- Keep the key information to bullet points - this is easy on the eye, clear and quick to assess exactly what you have done.
- When writing up the bullet points make sure each line starts with a different word i.e. "Designed" "Created" "Reduced" "Achieved" - keep it interesting.
- Use active words - achieved, drove, lead, headed, devised or passionate, driven, listener etc.
- Remember to back up general statements with facts and evidence.

In the UK it is not necessary to include a photo - unless you are specifically asked to include.

This tends to be fairly standard in some European Countries.

Write down three key achievements to include on your curriculum vitae:

_____

_____

_____

_____

_____

_____

_____

_____

_____

_____

_____

CHAPTER FOUR

Preparation before the Interview

The day of the interview is approaching

Interview Preparation is the key to increasing your chances of being hired.

Great news.....you've been invited to interview! First you get nervous with excitement and anticipation and then you're just plain nervous!!

Being nervous is normal and most people will experience this at some stage in their career history.

A good interviewer will be expecting some candidates to be nervous and will do their best to build rapport at the early stages and help calm you down.

Being nervous is a good sign that you consider this interview to be important and it's great that you are taking it seriously.

Interviewers generally want to get the best out of you to fully understand what you can offer the organisation.

It's no good if you are a bag of nerves, cannot talk properly, shake and freeze! How can they make a proper and fair assessment if they fuel your state!

Lots of interview preparation and a very clear vision of what you want to communicate and get across in the interview are absolutely essential – start to believe you are going to be and do your very best.

Preparation is as much about gathering information on the job, as it is about preparing yourself to communicate effectively about your skills, knowledge and types and levels of experiences.

Job Description

Ask for a Job Description – this will clearly define what you need to demonstrate at the interview and help with your interview preparation.

Go through every point – tasks, responsibilities, accountabilities, skills, knowledge and qualifications and provide evidence to support each point.

What's the difference between the job description and the person's specification? **The Job Description** outlines the tasks and duties – what you will be doing on a daily basis. **The Person Specification** describes the skills, knowledge and behaviours needed to perform the duties and tasks.

It's important that you go through each point on the job description and make notes about how you meet this criteria and what you've done recently to demonstrate these skills and competencies etc.

Key items that may be on the Job Description & Person Specification

✓ Job Responsibilities (Duties & Tasks, Accountabilities & Responsibilities, Job Content etc.)

✓ Person Specification – Essential & Desirable (skills, knowledge, types of experience, qualifications, training certificates.)

✓ Behavioural competencies (we'll cover these in more detail later.)

✓ Key Performance Indicators

✓ Compliance, regulation or legislation relating to this role

✓ Relationships – clients and internal customers, suppliers, other departments, divisions and provides, agents etc.

Interview Format

Ask about the format of the interview. Will it be a "Getting to know you" style interview or will it be a "Competency style" interview or will it be an "Assessment Centre" style interview. This is important for you to prepare appropriately.

Check out the different interview types in the next chapter.

Company Website

Check out the company website – always look at the website, mission and vision, values, business strategy, CEO's speech, and latest news.

Usually you can go direct to the careers page and find out what it's like to work at the organisation. There may also be some employee profiles on this page and you can get a feel of the company values etc.

The Interviewers

Check out the interviewers on LinkedIn – this is often used as a business card online these days. This will give you the person's background and where they have worked before.

It's also useful for starting a conversation with the interviewers and generates ideas for questions to ask at the end of the interview.

Plan your Journey

Location, location, location! Plan the route and if possible check out any alternatives if there are problems on the day. Check the trains, buses and planes before starting your journey.

No excuses if you get lost but if the train/bus/plane is running late phone and let them know – so don't forget to take a contact name and number!

Write down three skills, knowledge and types of experience you can contribute to an organisation:

_____
_____
_____
_____
_____
_____
_____
_____
_____
_____
_____

CHAPTER FIVE

Types of Interviews

Types of Interviews

Okay great news you've been invited to attend an interview.

There are several different interview types – unstructured, structured (we'll discuss this method later), panel interviews, assessment centres etc.

Unstructured Interview

I usually refer to these types of interviews as a "chat" or a "Getting to know you" – can you tell I'm not a big fan of this method!?! I worked in a Bank in the City of London for six years and it seemed to be common practise to meet with candidates in the local coffee shop.

Okay it's very sociable and creates an informal setting and I'm sure both candidate and interviewer have a relaxed conversation. However, the risks are potentially increased when you engage casually as you could "innocently" share inappropriate information.

There's no guarantee of confidentiality or data protection if you are in the middle of a busy public place.

Also bear in mind there's no guarantee your current manager or work colleagues don't walk in and sit on the table next to you. Awkward!! Embarrassing!! Or worse they spot you but you don't see them....say good bye to that promotion!

Keep all this in mind – it's still an interview so behave professionally at all times. It's essential you listen to what is being asked – this isn't necessarily a time to show off. If they give you instructions and ask for specific, concise answers you best stick to the objective.

Panel Interview

Panel interviews do have a tendency to fill candidates with dread and fear! They can be a daunting experience for candidates particularly if they are a bit rusty at the whole interview process.

Fake it, until you make it!

Act confidently - you'll be surprised how many people do this all the time. Be yourself and be genuine and be true to your values however, visualise the best case scenario and visualise the interview going successfully.

Preparation is the Key

Find out as much as possible about the process of the interview and the style of questions. It's okay to want to prepare and ask questions about the process - this demonstrates that you are taking this seriously, even before you go to the interview.

It also shows you are genuinely interested in the job and want to make a good impression.

Who's the audience?

Find out who is on the interview panel and their role in the organisation. Use LinkedIn to review the interviewer's background and employment history. Don't forget to build a rapport with everyone on the panel.

You may wish to give slightly more eye contact time to the person who asked the question however, you should still try to direct your comments to everyone.

Take Responsibility

Take responsibility for the things you have control over. Make sure you are smartly dressed and present yourself in the most professional manner, from the moment you enter the building through security to signing in at reception.

Keep Focused & Keep Calm!

Keep reminding yourself they invited you to attend an interview. They liked your CV, background, skills, knowledge and want to hear more.

Assessment Centres

Assessment centres are very successful methods of selecting the best talent – mainly because you have the opportunity to take part in a number of different selection methods.

It gives you a chance to take part in a number of very different activities such as ability tests, group exercises, role plays, presentations or the traditional interview. So if you prefer traditional interviews and perform well when presenting but really don't like ability tests then you still have plenty of opportunity to demonstrate lots of skills, knowledge and capability in your preferred methods.

If you are just about to graduate, you'll probably be expecting to take part in an Assessment Centre or two.

Here's my useful guide and tips to help you to prepare for that important day.

The advantage of an assessment event is that candidates have many different opportunities to succeed.

Not everyone is good at all types of assessment. Some people enjoy tests; others don't. Some people enjoy role play or group exercises and others prefer case studies or a traditional face to face interview.

Typical Assessment Centre Exercises

- Group Exercise
- Role Play
- Ability Tests
- Personality Questionnaires
- In Tray Exercise
- Presentation Exercise
- Case Studies

Group Interview tips: Improve your performance.

Listen carefully to the instructions and read all the information you are given throughout the day thoroughly.

Stay motivated and focused throughout the day. It's a tough day - so make sure you've had an early night and plenty of sleep the day before!

Remember you are being measured against predetermined criteria - not necessarily against another candidate, so try not to be in too much competition against your fellow candidates.

Work with others on the assessment day, encourage others to participate, voice their opinion and ask them questions to demonstrate you are actively listening - remember you are not in competition with them on the day or during the exercises.

Typical Criteria:

- Team working skills
- Communication skills
- Time Management
- Listening skills
- Motivation & enthusiasm
- Data analysis skills
- Decision Making skills
- Integrity
- Influencing skills
- Creativity & Innovation
- Leadership skills

Review the criteria the assessors will be measuring throughout the assessment centre - check out these typical behavioural competencies and the associated positive indicators.

We will cover Behavioural Competencies and how to prepare for this type of interview in Chapter Eight.

Things to avoid at an Assessment Centre

- Don't rail road over your peers - this is not demonstrating team working skills or leadership!
- Don't keep interrupting others when they are expressing their opinions - this will be noted!
- Don't lose track of time - volunteer or nominate someone in the group to keep an eye on the clock. Remember time is money in business!
- Don't ignore the quieter people in the group - try to involve everyone in the discussions.
- Don't focus on the Assessors - focus your full attention on the tasks.
- Don't forget to smile and enjoy the experience – even if you don't get through it's a fantastic experience and you may learn something valuable about yourself and others.

Telephone Interviews

There are two main types of telephone interview. The screening in and screening out telephone interview and the full competency style interview.

Globalisation, Advanced Technology and the war for talent means employers now attract and source candidates from much further afield.

Candidates from across Europe are particularly attracted to working in the City of London, as it's one of the financial centres of the world. As a consequence telephone interviews and video conferences are becoming the norm.

The telephone interview is a convenient, cost saving and time saving method of interviewing candidates in any location. It saves the candidate and organisation the cost of travel, sometimes over night accommodation or flights and saves a huge amount of time.

Find a quiet place

Make sure you find somewhere quiet, where there's no risk of being interrupted during the call. It's easy to get distracted during the interview and this may affect rapport.

This is one of the most basic phone interview tips.

You'll be surprised how many candidates go to a noisy park, have children screaming in the background or even continue to drive! That's an absolute no-no. Pull over and find a lay by!

Use your listening skills

Make sure you really listen to the question and allow gaps during your explanations for the interviewer to ask for clarification.

You don't want to talk for a long time just for the interviewer to tell you that isn't relevant for the job!

Take your notes with you

This is one of the advantages of having a phone interview. It's great to have a few bullet points to remind you of some examples you've prepared earlier.

Try not to write down everything and don't read straight from the notes. Again you may get distracted searching through lots of pages of information and this will surely affect the flow of the conversation.

For example, if you are asked why you are attracted to the job and you have to refer to notes, the interviewer may think you are not genuine. Your reasons should come from the heart....not a piece of paper!

Don't cheat

If you are being tested, for example, the interviewer will be asking technical questions. Don't be tempted to cheat by typing the question into a search engine!! I love Google but this is not the time.

The interviewer will hear you typing, the silent pause between the question and answer will be too long and you will get very distracted.

If you really don't know the answer you may well struggle in the job too and this can be very stressful to work in a job where you cannot meet the daily demands.

Preparation is the key

Some candidates make the mistake of thinking a telephone interview is much easier than a face to face. However, you are relying on only one of your five senses - listening skills.

Communication is mostly non-verbal and you'll be missing all this additional information from the interviewer's body language. So you really have to concentrate and focus on what's being asked.

Psychometric Tests (Ability Tests & Personality Questionnaires)

Psychometric testing can be a very valuable additional tool to an organisation if used appropriately and by qualified individuals.

What are the different types of psychometric tests available? The most commonly used tests are the Verbal Reasoning and Numerical Ability tests however there are many different technical tests to suit many different types of jobs.

These tests can be used as a screening in and out tool if they are expecting high volumes of applicants or they are setting particularly high standards of ability to a specific job.

Also widely used is the Personality Questionnaire – this is not a test. (There should be no right or wrong when assessing someone's personality - okay I acknowledge we could debate this subject!!)) and personality questionnaires should not be used in isolation.

Personality Questionnaires are not an indication of someone's ability or competence – it's assessing a candidates work style preferences.

This is not a screening in or out tool to be used prior to interview like ability tests above. It is however a great tool to generate further discussions and assessment during a structured interview.

Don't try to answer the questionnaire in a way you think the employer wants. There are many similar questions that are phrased differently to assess how consistently you have answered throughout the questionnaire.

So it's very important and in your interest to answer quickly and honestly otherwise you will be caught out!

Behavioural Competency Interviews (Structured Interviews)

We'll discuss Behavioural Competency Interviews in Chapter Eight.

Write down how you can prepare for the different types of interviews:

_____

_____

_____

_____

_____

_____

_____

_____

_____

_____

_____

_____

CHAPTER SIX

Motivational Fit

Motivational Fit

Recruiting managers will be very interested in the fit of the candidate into their team, department, the job and the company.

So they will be very interested in assessing your motivational fit, this includes: job fit, team fit and organisational or cultural fit.

Job Fit

The extent to which tasks, activities, accountabilities and responsibilities available in the job are consistent with the tasks, activities and responsibilities that result in personal satisfaction and the degree to which the work itself is personally satisfying.

Organisational & Cultural Fit

The extent to which an organisation's management style, operating principles, values are consistent with the type of environment that matches personal values and provides career satisfaction.

The recruiter or hiring manager will be gathering information about the following aspects

- Aspects of work that motivates or interests a person (likes or enjoys)

- Aspects that de-motivate or frustrate or even annoy, cause dislike or disinterest

- Aspects that would be missed if not present

- Aspects that a person is happy to avoid

Motivational Fit – key information sequence

- When candidates were most satisfied or dissatisfied with their work/organisation / situation and specifically – What was satisfying or dissatisfying

- When – identify a time when he/she was most / least satisfied

- What – the person was doing or experiencing that made them feel satisfied / dissatisfied

- Why – was the situation satisfying or dissatisfying

Managers will be looking to assess the following

- ✓ Identify occasions when the candidate has been most/least satisfied
- ✓ Identify what the candidate was doing to make them most satisfied/dissatisfied and the reasons why?
- ✓ Pull & Push Factors – reasons for deciding to join an organisation and reasons for leaving are all of interest to the hiring manager. Pull factors attract candidates to the job and push factors are reasons for leaving the current organisation.
- ✓ Compensation package - pay rates, salary expectations, benefits, rewards, recognition
- ✓ Training & Development / Career Opportunities / Career Paths – this is an important factor that attracts certain candidates to a role. Can the company / organisation satisfy this need?
- ✓ Personal Values align with the Company's values and principles

Write down three things that motivate you and three that de-motivate you at work:

_____

_____

_____

_____

_____

_____

_____

_____

_____

_____

CHAPTER SEVEN

Commonly asked Questions

Top Ten Common Questions

1. Why are you thinking of moving on?

The interviewer will be looking for hints of motivational fit to the job, culture and team.

The reasons for moving on from an organisation are extremely important to the next employer - so think carefully how you are going to answer this question and what you are willing to share at this stage.

2. Why are you interested in this job?

This should come from the heart - if there are particular parts or tasks in the job you most enjoy explain your reasons.

If you cannot explain or don't know then how can you expect an employer to guess! I would suspect you've not really given it much thought.

3. What are your strengths?

Not the most effective question for assessing your skills - as it's only your opinion on yourself. You're going to paint the best picture of course.

However, this is still commonly asked and it's worth having some prepared statements.

I would suggest if you want to be different and stand out that you back up what you claim with a brief specific example...but don't show off - no one likes a show off!

4. What are your weaknesses?

The positive spin on this question is "What are your developments?"

You absolutely must prepare an answer for this one - it's a question that could potentially affect your performance throughout the rest of the interview.

Get the balance right here. Think of skills or knowledge that are not essential requirements (or you'll be screening yourself out of a job!) but are desirable (which means it's an advantage but we can offer training) and that would give you a great opportunity to learn.

Be careful making statements like "My biggest weakness is being a perfectionist!" Good recruiters hate that one! Or "My biggest weakness is not being able to say no!"

5. What are your career aspirations for the next 3, 4 or 5 years?

There's really no right or wrong answer here however, again be prepared to be asked this question.

Be honest and true to yourself - if you are ambitious then show it and vice versa if you are not particularly career orientated and don't want to head up the department then that's fine.

Organisations will need and want a mixture of different career minded individuals and it is best you are honest up front - it avoids tears later!

6. Tell me about yourself?

As a seasoned recruiter I hate this one and in today's litigious market it's also a risky question to ask candidates because it could bring up very personal details and stuff not suitable to discuss in an interview.

Again it's a question still asked by old school managers whom in fairness just want to relax you and start building that all important rapport.

7. Talk me through your greatest achievement to date?

This is a great opportunity for you to shine and stand out from the others.

Make sure you explain exactly what you did in the situation, your tasks and actions and what results and impact this had on you and for the organisation.

There's much more information about structured interviews in Chapter Eight.

8. How would your manager describe you at work?

Another great opportunity to share the positive opinions with the interviewer - remember you are in control of how much you share at this stage.

However, be very careful if you are trying to hide your true feelings about a given manager or hide a particularly difficult relationship.

The interviewer may pick up on your non verbal body language or emotional leakage as we recruiters like to say!!

9. How would your colleagues describe you at work?

Same as above....it's an opinion based answer and easy to bluff this one but watch out for that uncomfortable body language if you are trying to hide something!

10. What is your ideal job and working environment?

The interviewer is probably assessing your motivational fit to the job and the culture.

I would not suggest you fake this one - it's as important to you as it is to the company that you fit into the organisations culture, values and core principles.

Therefore, when you are researching the company review their values and try to get a feel if this is a place you would be happy working and match your values to the companies.

General Questions

We think it's worth mentioning these general questions that sometimes get asked at the beginning of the process to manage everyone's expectations.

Sometimes they are asked at the end of the process to help with the next and final stage – the offer negotiations. Don't be mistaken – if you are being asked these questions during the interview stage then this isn't the time to negotiate.

Give these general questions some consideration and think about how and what you want the outcome to be.

✓ **Current Salary & Benefits** it's important to find out what money value your current benefits equal – we've interviewed candidates before with very generous pension contributions from their employer and this needs to be covered in your calculations of salary expectations.

✓ **Salary Expectations** if you are taking a drop in salary be prepared to justify and explain the reasons why are you willing to accept a decrease. Unless you know the budget is lower then don't be too quick to lower your salary.

✓ **Notice Period or Availability** Be absolutely honest about when you can start work in terms of the legal / formal notice period or anything that could prevent you starting when expected.

✓ **Holidays booked** Again be honest about holidays you've booked and paid for and don't want to lose – even if it's an extended holiday. New Employers would rather know so they can prepare – this shouldn't necessarily change their decision about you unless the job is temporary and there's a need to commit to a short fixed term period.

✓ **Are you eligible to work in the UK?** At some point in the process you will be asked whether you are eligible to work in the UK. If you require a visa to work in the UK it is your responsibility to understand the terms and conditions of your residence and work entitlement.

Write down how you will answer these questions:

_____

_____

_____

_____

_____

_____

_____

_____

_____

_____

_____

CHAPTER EIGHT

Understanding & Preparing for Behavioural Competency Interviews

What are behavioural competencies?

There are several definitions to consider. Generally it's about demonstrating and having the ability to perform a specific role.

"A competence is a standardised and measurable requirement for an individual to correctly perform a specific job. It is a combination of knowledge, skills and behaviour which may be utilised to improve performance."

During the interview recruiters are attempting to predict the future behaviour and capability of that candidate in the job role.

The best method to be able to do this with as much certainty as possible is by gathering evidence from that candidate's past using the Behavioural Competency Style Questions.

Why use Behavioural Competency Questions?

✓ Past behaviour is a good predictor of future behaviour

✓ Excellent tool for gathering job related information & evidence

✓ Excellent tool for assessing a candidate's potential ability to perform in the role

✓ A useful tool for giving feedback – successful or unsuccessful

✓ Encourages objective decision making

If you believe the research on Predictive Validity (a measurement of how well a method predicts the future performance) then you'll understand that the more structured the interview and the more relevant information that is gathered during the interview the more likely the hiring manager is able to get closer to selecting the best fitting candidate.

If they just relied on a CV or just having an informal "chat" with a candidate then it's more likely going to decrease the chance of getting the right fit.

The above hopefully gives you an insight into how and why recruiters use the behavioural competency style questions.

Here are some common Behavioural Competencies:

- Communication & presentation skills

- Interpersonal skills

- Decision making skills

- Customer / Client Focused Orientation

- Planning & organisation skills

- Time management

- Prioritising skills

- Results orientation

- Teamwork skills

- Project management

- Resilience & tough mindedness

- Driven & results orientated

- People management, people development, performance management

These are just a few examples of behavioural competencies – there are many more!

Each behavioural competency has its own set of positive and negative indicators.

These are essential in being able to measure if someone is actually competent in a particular behaviour.

These indicators are collected as evidence during the interview.

Interviewers will be looking and probing for these indicators throughout the interview.

Behavioural Competency Examples

It's worth having a look at several examples of behavioural competencies, the definition and the associated positive and negative indicators.

When you prepare your examples keep these positive indicators in mind – ask yourself are you providing enough evidence of your capability.

Customer Service Orientation

Customer service is the ability to provide excellent support to customers before, during and after a purchase of products or services.

+ Positive Indicators	- Negative Indicators
Is able to build strong relationships with new and existing customers. Keeps in regular contact with clients and their business/industry/sector and maintains good working relationships to ensure they understand their specific requirements. Keeps up to date with market / sector knowledge – through publications, seminars and legislation. Is able to respond to complaints in a timely and professional manner. Is able to investigate systems to determine route cause of issues or problems raised by the clients.	Lacks the ability or skills to build relationships. Doesn't talk or meet with clients on a regular basis. Doesn't keep up to date with market trends or is just not interested. Is not able to utilise systems to properly investigate issues or complaints. Is not able to utilise systems to maximise stored information and keep records up to date. Has shallow relationships with clients. Cannot predict future needs of the clients – due to lack of contact or interest or ability. Is not able to build rapport with new or existing customers.

Communication

Speaks clearly, fluently and in a compelling manner to both individuals and groups. Writes in a clear and concise manner, using appropriate grammar, style and language for the reader.

+ Positive Indicators	- Negative Indicators
Confident, unhesitant and articulate when talking.	Lacks confidence when talking.
Uses appropriate language for audience and situation.	Speaks too fast or too slowly.
Doesn't use jargon carelessly.	Uses inappropriate jargon.
Adapts style to the audience.	Tends to stick to one style of communication.
Expressive and interesting to listen to.	Seldom varies tone or intonation.
Understands how to keep the audience attention, e.g. uses summary and restatement.	No structure.
Writes fluently and concisely.	Uses closed or negative body language.
Structures communication.	Does not check the message was understood.
Ensure the message is understood by the recipient by asking appropriate questions.	Tendency to waffle or go off at a tangent – losing audience attention.
Is comfortable using a variety of communication methods.	Does not adapt style or method of communication to suit the situation.
	Does not gain audience attention or engagement.

Planning and Organising

Developing programmes of action to accomplish objectives and results. Organise and schedules events, activities and resources. Set up and monitors timescales and plans.

+ Positive Indicators	Negative Indicators
Makes time for planning.	Disorganised, unstructured and no clear priorities.
Prepares in advance for short and medium term.	Does not allow time for planning.
Realistic about timescales.	Rarely prepares or draws up schedule.
Prioritises work accurately.	Rarely monitors progress.
Plans for changing circumstances.	Misses deadlines.
Systematic in approach.	Is not able to work without distraction.
Creates effective schedules, sets and monitors objectives.	Is not able to accurately assess the time to perform certain tasks.
Reviews schedule regularly.	Unable to adjust to changing priorities.
Is able to adapt to changing timescales and business priorities.	Lacks enthusiasm for completing and finishing tasks or objectives.
Thrives on challenging tasks and objectives.	
Enjoys taking responsibility for task completion.	

Problem Solving and Analysis

Analyses issues and breaks them down into their component parts. Makes systematic and rational judgements based on relevant information.

+ Positive Indicators	- Negative Indicators
Asks questions to gather pertinent information.	Sees problem only as a whole.
Distinguishes fact from opinion.	Misinterprets information, draws inappropriate conclusions.
Identifies the main components of a problem.	Swayed by intuition, takes unnecessary risks.
Makes rational or logical judgements.	Slow to grasp or solve problems.
Bases decisions on relevant information.	Analyses things at an inappropriate level of detail.
Analyses facts, figures or information looking for trends.	Is unable to interrupt data as a whole and therefore, makes decisions in isolation.
Knows when more information is required.	Is unable to identify trends or patterns in volumes of data.
Integrates data from different sources.	Arrives at conclusions without reviewing the relevant data.
Breaks down complex issues/problems, to smaller parts. Identifies implications and casual links.	Is unable to break down the data into manageable chunks.

Influence and Persuasiveness

Influences, convinces or impresses others in a way that results in acceptance, agreement or behaviour change. Uses internal and external contacts to build relationships and improve competitive position.

+ Positive Indicators	- Negative Indicators
Gives facts benefits and implications of an argument.	Fails to gain commitment from others.
Changes the opinion/direction of others.	Rarely changes the opinion/direction of others.
Gains commitment and agreement to own point of view.	Needs help in selling ideas/opinions.
Knows how to lobby effectively.	Limited ability to promote own ideas.
Sways others with counter arguments.	Does not overcome objections.
Handles objections convincingly, does not back down when challenged.	Backs down easily or changes view when challenged.
Uses different approaches and adapts to cues.	Is uncomfortable during intensive negotiations.
Is comfortable managing negotiations.	Is not able to achieve a win-win outcome.

Personal Motivation

Commits self to work hard towards goals. Shows enthusiasm and career commitment. The drive and determination to get things done, to move things forward, to achieve, to get results, and to do things better.

+ Positive Indicators	- Negative indicators
Shown drive and determination to get results.	Less motivated than others to achieve.
Achieves goals and then seeks new ones.	Prefers simple tasks.
Readily tackles demanding tasks or takes on new work.	Gives up when challenged or disappointed.
Looks forward to or enjoys a challenge.	Complacent about achievements.
Produces outstanding results and exceeds targets regularly.	Only acquires new skills when pushed.
Seeks career progression or sets career goals.	Prefers not to take on new responsibilities.
Is determined to succeed.	Sets easy targets and personal objectives.
Is enthusiastic and calm.	Rarely exceeds targets.
Is career orientated and ambitious.	Lacks enthusiasm.

Resilience

Maintains optimism, energy and effectiveness in the face of sustained pressure. Remains calm, stable and quickly recovers from disruptive change or failure.

+ Positive Indicators	- Negative Indicators
Copes with disappointments/setbacks and keeps going.	Allows disappointments to become overwhelming.
Deals with pressure calmly.	Panics under pressure.
Rarely tense for long, able to relax.	Gloomy in outlook.
Optimistic and resilient.	Tends to find it difficult to bounce back.
Keeps control in stressful situations.	Gets things out of proportion.
Keeps difficulties in perspective.	Allows stress to get to them.
Is self-controlled.	Too sensitive to criticism.
Not overly sensitive to criticism.	Is not able to cope under pressure.
Is approachable.	Takes criticism personally.
Approaches tasks with energy.	Tends to dwell on failures or set-backs.
Is able to move on quickly from set-backs.	

Star Model

The most commonly used method of assessing a candidate and evaluating the data gathered after the interview is the **S.T.A.R technique**.

```
                    S.T.A.R MODEL

SITUATION = Explain the scenario or story

TASK = Explain the tasks and responsibilities

ACTION = Explain the actions taken

RESULTS = Outcomes, benefits, and impact
```

When you are asked in the interview to provide a specific example from your academic studies, work history and background – these are the rules to follow to ensure you stand out from the crowd!

Remember to be specific and talk through an example from the past.

The STAR process is a well known, tried and tested method of gathering information and data during the interview.

It provides a structure and framework to probe for specific information and consequently to ask the most appropriate follow up questions.

The good news for candidates is that you can use the same method to prepare specific examples.

Situation or Task

Describe the situation that you were in or the task that you needed to accomplish.

You need to describe a specific event or situation, (not a generalised description) of what you have done in the past.

Be sure to give enough detail for the interviewer to understand. This situation can be from a previous job, from a volunteer experience, or any relevant event.

If you're a graduate and have no previous work experience to draw on, there are probably lots of opportunities you have had throughout your studies to demonstrate behavioural competencies i.e. team working skills, presentation skills, research skills, planning and organising skills and the list goes on....

Actions you took

Describe the actions you took and be sure to keep the focus on what you did and your responsibilities.

Even if you are discussing a group project or effort, describe what you did - not the efforts of the team.

Don't tell the interviewer what you might do, tell them what you did.

Results you achieved

What happened? How did the event end? What did you accomplish? What did you learn?

Be sure to let the interviewer know the reasons why the result might be negative, i.e. market changes, budgets cut, specification changes, etc.

The reason for asking candidates to provide a specific example from the past is because past behaviour is a good predictor of future behaviour.

Remember that this style of interviewing is designed to give you the candidate the best opportunity to demonstrate key competencies and for that reason give you a better chance of getting the job you want and deserve.

How to prepare examples

Imagine you are watching yourself in the situation and start to describe the situation or story.

You are attempting to think of the detail on the behaviour you demonstrated during that event and not detail about the process or the context of the event itself.

A good STAR is a behavioural example which contains all elements of the STAR. The result may be positive or negative; both are valid examples of behaviour.

Try not to use the same examples for several competencies. The interviewer needs to gain a good understanding of your exposure to different and wider ranging situations.

To review your examples, consider the following:

Avoid generalisations – rather than specific information about what you actually did there is a tendency to generalise about what you usually do in such situations.

Words to be aware of are, "would", "could", "usually", "always", "generally", "tend" to or "often".

Provide Specific Examples

The key to the successful application of the behavioural competency question is to make sure you have given a specific example. You must take the recruiter back into that event, project, objective or task. Being specific and clear in the interview is absolutely essential.

Interviewers will want to understand exactly what you have done and your capability, what you have achieved in previous roles, your specific level of skills (basic, intermediate or advanced) your competence to perform certain tasks and the types of experiences you have gained throughout your career.

The challenge for candidates with these types of questions is thinking of an example during the interview – that's when the pressure and nerves might kick in and your mind suddenly goes completely blank!! It's therefore important to spend time thinking and preparing for this style of interview.

Avoid Generalised Statements

Generalised statements that sound good and use positive words (For example, "I'm proactive", "I'm excellent at prioritising", "I'm extremely organised"), provide no specific evidence to the interviewer.

To avoid this situation happening make sure you provide <u>specific examples</u> and demonstrate that you have applied this knowledge previously.

Situation or task questions

Below are some examples of probing questions you might be asked during the interview. Start to think about the answers when you prepare your specific examples.

- ✓ What was the main objective?

- ✓ What were the circumstances surrounding? What was the context for this?

- ✓ Does an example of that situation stand out?

- ✓ What were the problems you were trying to address?

- ✓ What were the specific challenges at this time?

Action questions

- ✓ Exactly what did you do?

- ✓ Describe specifically how you did that.

- ✓ What did you do first / second / next?

- ✓ Talk me through the steps you took.

- ✓ What was your specific contribution?

- ✓ What did you do to meet the deadline?

- ✓ What did you say when that happened?

- ✓ Was there anything in hindsight you didn't do?

- ✓ What tasks did you take responsibility for?

- ✓ Who were you accountable to during the project?

- ✓ How was your involvement valuable to the business?

- ✓ What impact did your expertise have on the project?

Result questions

✓ What was the end result? (Don't just say "good" explain the impact of your actions. Did it save time or money for the organisation? Did you develop new skills and progress in your career?)

✓ How did it work out? How did you know it had worked?

✓ What results were directly related to what you did?

✓ How would you describe its success?

✓ How do you know that what you did was effective?

✓ What feedback did you receive?

✓ What were the criteria for success?

✓ If the project was unsuccessful explain the reasons why?

Final Thought on Behavioural Competencies

As you can appreciate there are hundreds of different questions that could be asked by the interviewers and you may not be able to predict those questions.

It's not good use of your time to prepare for individual competency questions you don't even know are going to be asked. General questions mentioned in the previous chapter yes but not various competency questions.

Therefore, my suggestion would be to focus your time on preparing really good, specific examples.

Pick the most common competencies – planning and organising, communication, interpersonal skills, team work, building relationships or customer orientation.

As mentioned above the examples should include the situation, actions, tasks and punchy results and outcomes S.T.A.R!

By having five or six really good specific and detailed examples you'll be prepared to answer far more questions by focusing on the specific competency the recruiter is trying to assess.

For example, if the competency is communication skills – you can pick out how you prepared the communication, which methods of communication you used and how you ensured your message was understood in one of your prepared examples.

If the competency is planning and organising, the same example could be used but with a different emphasis on how you planned out the tasks, the time and you met deadlines and prioritised.

Note – it's not a good idea to use the same example over and over again in the interview.

That's why having five or six gives you an opportunity to answer several different competencies with a different example.

Look at this specific example:

Situation: I had been working with a Senior Manager to assist him with his recruitment since I joined the company in 2008.

In 2010 he had to manage out his poorly performing deputy head and was left managing 25 direct reports across four teams.

He also had two members of his team move internally and two leave the organisation and one new vacancy. This left him with five vacancies.

Tasks & Actions: Having built up a very good relationship with the manager and gained really good knowledge of the type of employees that fit the department, the skill set and knowledge requirements I offered to conduct all of the first stage interviewing for him.

At first he felt he was losing a little control and was resistant to letting go.

I explained that this would save him time and that he would still receive all of the information gathered at the interviews and would still be the ultimate decision maker.

I made it clear that no decision would be made without his involvement.

He would still be able to challenge my recommendations on candidates going forward or not and he could still meet candidates at the final stages.

Results: By conducting the first stage interviews it saved hours of management time and reduced the indirect cost of the hiring process.

I booked regular meetings where I would give the manager updates - producing written score charts, graphs and summary notes on all candidates interviewed and reasons for taking forward or rejecting.

This resulted in the manager still feeling part of the process and very much involved in the decision making but freeing him up to spend time on business critical activities.

Personally it gave me the ability to increase my knowledge of the department and much more knowledge of the job requirements and gave me a satisfying role in the process. **End of example.**

Okay you get the idea with the example. I could add even more detail – how did I communicate with the manager? How did I put together the interview questions and format? What was the assessment criteria? How did I manage all the interviews in a timely manner? Etc.

Look at the questions below and how the specific example above could be tweaked to answer all of these by emphasising slightly different parts of the example.

Negotiation or Persuasion skills:

- Talk us through a time when you had to persuade a manager about your support or services?

Results Driven & Personal Effectiveness:

- Tell us a time when you added real value to the business?

- Describe an occasion when you had to manage a high turnover in one department?

Planning & Organising skills:

- Tell us a time when you had to carefully plan and organise a high workload?

Building & Maintaining Relationships:

- Talk us through a time you improved your relationship with an internal client and tell us how you achieve a positive outcome?

If any one of these questions came up in the interview I could draw upon that one example to talk through and focus on that particular element.

It's likely you'll be asked about three to four different behavioural questions during one interview. Therefore, having about five or six really good specific and detailed examples will be sufficient.

As recommended previously it's not good to use the same example over and over again – because it doesn't give the hiring manager an idea of the depth of your knowledge and experience.

You may be able to justify using the same example twice but it's not suggested any more than twice.

Therefore, don't worry too much about the questions – worry and focus your time and effort on thinking about the specific examples and you'll be fine in the interview!

This is why keeping a works journal or diary will help you build up lots of specific examples and keep them fresh in your mind – not just for the next interview but for your yearly or half yearly appraisal too.

Write down three complete specific examples to demonstrate three different competencies – use the S.T.A.R. Model:

_____

_____

_____

_____

_____

_____

_____

_____

_____

_____

_____

CHAPTER NINE

How to Market your Value Proposition

How to Market your Value Proposition

In today's competitive market you need to differentiate yourself and stand out from the others. This means making sure you know how to market yourself. Typically organisations receive high volumes of applications – particularly the big corporate companies.

If you are currently employed look around the office and identify the people you admire, get the promotions and get the attention of management.

Passionate and Driven

What characteristics or traits do they have in common? They are passionate about their job, the team's goals and are engaged in the company's values and objectives. They are keen, enthusiastic, energetic, and act with excitement about taking on tasks and new projects.

They have drive and want to succeed. They are or act confidently and are very good communicators.

Knowledgeable

Successful employees are knowledgeable in several key areas – this makes you a valuable asset to the organisation, the department and team.

Successful people network internally and externally to ensure they build a contact base with breadth and depth.

Be an Expert

Successful employees are also experts in their field – this may seem like a contradiction to my first point but you can be an expert or a go to person in a specialist subject and have other key related skills.

For example, if you were a Credit Analyst you may well specialise in Project Finance or Corporate Finance but have cash-flow analysis skills, scenario testing and presentation skills.

Promote yourself

Research shows that people who are confident in selling and promoting their skills and value are more likely to get the job, get promoted and get ahead.

No one else is going to manage your career – trust me I'm an In-House Recruiter! Even your biggest fan or a proud manager is not waking up and putting your career development at the top of their list of things to do that day!

Start getting comfortable about "selling" your value to an organisation.

**Write down three of your unique selling points
and reasons why they should offer you the job:**

_____

_____

_____

_____

_____

_____

_____

_____

_____

_____

_____

_____

CHAPTER TEN

Avoid Common Mistakes

The UK labour market has been very tough over the last five to six years and the competition for jobs is still challenging. I should know I've been working in the financial sector since the recession started in 2007 / 2008.

Employers have been able to set high standards and wait until they find the perfect candidate that meets all their demands – regardless whether it takes more time, they are more interested in the quality of the candidate than time to hire stats!

This is perfectly normal to have an employer's market during a downturn or a candidate driven market when jobs are buoyant. It's like the housing market, sometimes it's a buyer's market and other times it's a seller's market. It's no different in the job market.

The market is starting to change and we are seeing an increase in vacancies (albeit spread across different sectors). However you will still want to gain as much advantage over the other candidates (the competition!) as you can.

Lack of Research or Preparation

This first point might sound obvious or common sense – however, you'll be surprised how many candidates think they can wing it or win the interview with their personality alone.

Think about how much time and energy the manager or HR person has spent to get to the interview stage.

They have probably spent time designing and writing the job description, creating the job adverts, internally and possibly externally, briefed the recruitment agents, screened 100's of CVs if they've advertised direct (sometimes upwards of 500 CVs can be received for the big brands!), and spent time deciding on the selection process and questions for the interviews.

Therefore, it's only right that you spend some time prepping and reviewing the company website!

Once you are invited to interview start reviewing all the information you have been given and prepare to explain in detail specific examples from your experiences that match the requirements for the job.

Candidates are generally unprepared for the behavioural interview and do not provide adequate evidence of their competency during the interview. So focus on your achievements and how to present them in a concise but comprehensive manner.

Being Negative About the Last Employer or Your Boss

Everyone knows not to be negative in the interview but it's still surprising how many candidates don't properly prepare how they are going to respond, react and handle the associated questions.

Interviewers will ask – why are you looking to move on? What has triggered the interest to look for another job?

No one is saying you should lie – absolutely not. Just be prepared to answer the questions or you will put up the barriers, potentially feel uncomfortable and this will leak out in your body language.

The trouble with body language is it's down to the interpretation of the reader and can so easily be misinterpreted and then the interviewer will think you are trying to hide something negative. You do not want to leave any doubts in the interviewer's mind – as they are more likely not to progress your application to the next stage.

Too Comfortable During the Interview

There's a difference between building good rapport with the interviewer and getting too familiar.

Keep in mind it's an interview and if you are too casual during the interview how are you going to behave in the workplace. Of course this works both ways – if the interviewer is very familiar you may want to consider if this is a place you would feel comfortable working.

It's important to keep that professionalism throughout the interview process. Be your most professional self.

Exaggerating on Your CV

It's easy to think you can exaggerate on your CV – who's going to know or find out! However, if you are questioned during the interview to explain in detail how you accomplished a particularly impressive objective you better be prepared for some tough questioning.

It's difficult to keep up the pretence when there's question after question (probing) and you have to make it up on the spot – that's a lot of additional pressure you can do without.

Trust me, there are some managers and HR professionals that won't stop until they are satisfied they have all the evidence....whether or not you are grilled, you will definitely feel grilled!

Lack Passion or Motivation

The "any job" will do syndrome will not get you to second stage – if not the first stage cut short. Let's be realistic here and repeat my previous point – how much time has the manager, HR, the interviewer or the agency spent getting to the interview stage – then you turn up half hearted about the role.

Of course technical ability to do the job is important but once this is established managers will be looking for genuine reasons for your interest in working with them and in that particular organisation. Your motivational fit for the job, the department and the organisation makes the difference between you getting offered the job or someone else!

The golden thread running throughout these common mistakes is not being prepared. So be prepared to communicate and present yourself and your career background accurately and comprehensively. Be prepared to spend some time reviewing the various documents you've been given prior to the interview and spending some time reviewing the company website.

Write down how you are going to avoid these mistakes:

_____

_____

_____

_____

_____

_____

_____

_____

_____

_____

_____

CHAPTER ELEVEN

Offer Stage

Negotiating the Offer

You've been identified as the chosen candidate and it's time to talk about the offer.

Negotiation is an art. You need to go about it very carefully otherwise you will end up spoiling all the goodwill and brownie points you gained for yourself over the interview.

Unless there is a fixed package for the role in which you are applying, it is standard practice to discuss your terms and conditions at the end of an interview.

However, a lot of people feel uncomfortable to talk about money and what they want.

This need not be the case!

You can act in the situation by reading the orientation of the interviewer. If you can see that the company is keen then you do have a considerable amount of power!

Here are some tips and pointers on how to get what you think you are worth.

Only ever talk about pay and conditions from a position of strength. You don't want to start negotiating the package before they are sure of hiring you. Keep your eyes and ears open and get into the act only when you feel that the company wants you and is interested in employing you.

Unless you are requested to indicate your remuneration at application stage - putting that you want £20,000 and a car in your covering letter is not going to get you very far! Try to avoid talking about pay and conditions until as late as possible.

- Do not bring it up in your Cover Letter
- Do not bring it up in your Curriculum Vitae
- Try to avoid it at your first interview

Try to leave it as late as possible until you are in the room with a decision maker who has the authority and that's when you play your cards.

Do your homework and prepare beforehand. Just as you would prepare to answer interview questions you need to do some pre-work in order to discuss your terms and conditions as well.

Set a minimum worth for yourself and also an ideal maximum amount you would be happy with.

But the question is how do you determine these figures?

Ideally you would have some sort of idea as to the salary range and benefits package before you applied for the job.

Start by finding out the standard pay scale for the post you are applying for in the industry. Find out how good a pay master the company is and the different kinds of incentives and perks they provide to their employees.

If the salary said circa £30,000 for example you know that it needs to be around this figure.

What happens is that this figure would probably be median point of a salary scale so the range could go from £25,000 through to £35,000.

Ask yourself "Would I be happy with £25,000?" and "Am I worth £35,000?"

Go in with a figure that serves your expertise and experience right.

How to respond to the salary question

The time has come!

It is time to discuss your salary requirements.

Don't give up out rightly the figures you have in mind.

Make sure you know what you are playing with before getting into the number game.

Make the interviewer come out with their figure if you can manage.

Here is a great response to the question:

"What are your salary requirements?"

Response:

"This is the first time we have mentioned money, could you tell me what the salary range is for someone with my experience and qualifications?

What you are doing here is trying to reveal the salary range what the company has to play with. So you can see if it fits your scheme of things and accordingly you can quote your figure.

Your first objective is to get a salary range out on the table so that you can compare it to what you wanted.

When the salary range is revealed it is very important that you do not show any emotion whatsoever – whether you are delighted with the offer or not maintain a poker face!

- Pay close attention to your body language signals.

- Don't look too happy or too disappointed

- Maintain eye contact

- Do not fidget or move your legs

- Do not touch your face or hair

Just keep exactly the same posture and body position as you had before the salary range was revealed to you. Giving out subtle expressions at this stage is spoiling it all!

What to Do With the Salary Range

Now that the salary range has been revealed you have a number of options.

Let's assume that the salary range is £20,000 - £30,000

Accept

You can say "The upper end of the salary range is what I had in mind"

If you are happy with the range and it is what you want then there is nothing stopping you from agreeing to the offer there and then.

Bear in mind however that the range that the employer gives you is normally always open for negotiation at the top end. So don't succumb to it and try to get a higher figure. You never know, you could get it if you are a good catch for the company.

Counter bid

You can say "What I had in mind was £25,000 - £30,000"

You would put this counter offer in if the salary that you wanted was £25,000+

You will need to go over your USP's again to remind the employer why you are worth that little bit extra and what you will bring to their company.

Play it up with conviction for the desired impact!

Sit on the fence

You can say "Thanks for the figure. Could I have some time to think it over?"

This is a better option than rejecting the figures as in our last example below.

If the salary range is below what you expected it is better to take some time out to think through what it means for you and your family rather than express your dissatisfaction pronto.

It will also give the employer time to weigh up whether they are running the risk of losing you at this late stage; you never know they might just up the range considering the chances.

Reject the salary range

You can of course reject the range completely but we do not recommend this!

It is difficult to find a win-win situation for yourself and the company if you come flat out with that you do not want this position because of the salary alone.

If all the other factors appealed to you maybe something could be worked out, so steer clear of the complete rejection as you may not recover.

It is better to take time out and "sit on the fence" for a couple of days.

Closing the negotiations

Remember you are negotiating a win-win resolution – you are not trying to shift the "power" in your favour. This will only result in the company withdrawing the offer altogether. It's been done and if you haven't accepted the offer they can lawfully withdraw without any consequences. So be careful not to push it too far!

Be polite and professional throughout the process and remember to always take into consideration the bigger picture i.e. promotional opportunities, learning and development opportunities.

Always aim for a middle ground and decide what you are willing to compromise or trade. Some organisations, depending on the size, have a lot more flexibility on different benefits – such as holiday entitlements, earlier salary reviews and mid-year bonus and performance reviews.

Here are some facts to consider on both sides of the fence.

Candidates

As a candidate you are likely to be looking at your current or last salary and possibly the annual increases you didn't get.

You will be looking at the cost of living, the rent or mortgage or your personal situation (married, children etc).

Some of these factors are none of the employers' business but are very important to take into consideration.

- Current or last salary
- Lack of salary increases in the past – this is a new addition to this list of consideration given the recession
- What they feel they are worth or what their friends are earning (I kid you not!)
- Mortgage
- Rent
- Cost of living
- Financial commitments
- Family situation - children, schooling, etc.

Managers

Employers are considering salary levels against market norms, salaries of equivalent employees in their existing teams, internal comparisons and of course budget constraints.

Therefore, it's best to be clear on both sides before progressing through the interview process.

- Budgets & Headcount Allocations
- Internal Comparisons
- External Market Comparisons
- Salary level for the job role

Write down your criteria for deciding your salary expectations:

_____

_____

_____

_____

_____

_____

_____

_____

_____

_____

_____

Conclusion

I wrote this book to give you an insight into the recruitment process and take you behind the scenes to gain a better understanding of how you really can stand out from the hundreds of applicants and job seekers in today's highly competitive labour market.

I hope you have gained lots from the information shared and if you can apply the tools and techniques in your next job search it really will give you the advantage you deserve.

The very fact that you've bought this book indicates that you already value your career and are willing to invest in your personal development.

Remember the interview process is like playing a game – get to know and familiarise yourself with the rules to help you through the process and most of all have fun, learn and enjoy!

I'm not just an In-House Recruiter or Your Interview Coach – I've also been on the other side of the fence (or should I say the other side of the interview desk!) and have to go through the interview process like any other candidate! I still get a little nervous when I really want to land a particularly interesting job.

I've had to learn to deal with rejection like everyone else and this is key to managing your job search and career – it's inevitable that you will have to deal with rejection and the sooner you learn to cope with this the closer you'll get to landing the job of your dreams or as close as you can get!

Remember failure only happens when you give up trying! So keep going until you achieve your career goals.

I want to leave you with this final thought – Knowledge is power only when you apply the knowledge.

Read, learn and apply!

Apply the knowledge and Apply for that Job!

About the Author

Dawn Moss and her story: she left school as soon as she could (1984) - well actually it was a bit before the end of the last term!! She wanted to explore life and have fun rather than being stuck in a stuffy and boring class room! With two CSEs to her name she decided she would only be worthy of dead end, low skilled jobs. Her expectations and self esteem were set pretty low and that good old prophesy (that's the self fulfilling one!), gave her the results she expected and believed she deserved.

She mainly worked in shops and cleaned for a living. Don't get the wrong idea – she loved those jobs at the time and worked very hard, she was loyal, punctual and diligent (a few words there she wouldn't have even been able to spell back then!).

Dawn has since gained a 2:1 Honours Degree in Health Promotion (1995), qualified as a Human Resource Professional and gained Membership to the Chartered Institute of Personnel Development (2006). She has trained with SHL the leaders in Psychometrics and can administer and interpret psychometric ability tests and personality questionnaires. She has trained as a Personal and Career Coach and is a member of the Association of Coaching (2010).

Dawn has worked in a corporate blue chip environment for over a decade and now runs a coaching and training practice. She has coached and interviewed hundreds if not thousands of people during her career in Human Resources and as a Life & Career Coach and now wants to share what she believes to be vital and valuable information on interview skills for candidates.

Thank you for purchasing her book. Enjoy reading and learning and good luck in the next interview!!

Don't forget that we are here to help you with your recruitment questions – and we provide both one to one coaching and group workshops!

To get in touch, simply visit ©Your Interview Coach @ http://www.yourinterviewcoach.co.uk or email dawn@yourinterviewcoach.co.uk or call 07932 434 303

Acknowledgements

A big thank you to my managers and my colleagues over the last 12 years – this book would not have been possible without your support, guidance and the opportunity to gain experience and improve my skills and knowledge.

A big thank you to my business associates over the last 6 months – you've inspired me to share my knowledge and expertise with others. You've encouraged me to just do it!

And of course, a big thank you to you for purchasing my book!

If this information was useful please feel free to write a review – it just may help someone else to purchase the book.

© Your Interview Coach 2014

Invest in You & Your Career!

Resources & Useful Links

Recommended Recruitment Agencies:

NDK   www.ndkconsulting.co.uk

G Square HR   www.gsquaredhr.com

Prime Personnel   www.primeuk.com

Robert Walters   www.robertwalters.com

Morgan McKinley   www.morganmckinley.com

Hays   www.hays.co.uk

Robert Half   www.roberthalf.co.uk

Top Flight Personnel   www.topflightpersonnel.co.uk

Reed   www.reed.co.uk

Adecco & Office Angels   www.adecco.co.uk

Office Angels   www.office-angels.com

On-Line Job Boards

eFinancial Careers - Financial Sector

www.efinancialcareers.co.uk

Monster – General

www.monster.co.uk

Reed - Administration / Office

www.reed.co.uk

Totaljobs – General

www.totaljobs.com

The Lawyer - Legal Sector

www.thelawyer.com

Personnel Today - Human Resources Sector

www.personneltoday.com

Indeed – General

www.indeed.co.uk